Country Hits
2008 Edition

T0052961

CONTENTS

Alfred Publishing Co., Inc.
16320 Roscoe Blvd., Suite 100
P.O. Box 10003
Van Nuys, CA 91410-0003
alfred.com

ISBN-10: 0-7390-5635-2
ISBN-13: 978-0-7390-5635-6

Cover photograph: Concert Crowd © istockphoto.com/dwphotos

ANYWAY

Words and Music by
MARTINA McBRIDE, BRAD WARREN
and BRETT WARREN

Moderately slow ballad ♩ = 66

Verse 1:

1. You can spend your whole life build-ing some-thing from noth-ing. One storm can come and blow it all a-way. Build it an-y-way. You can chase a dream that

Anyway - 6 - 1

seems so out of reach,___ and you know it might___ not ev - er come___ your___

___ way. Dream it an - y - way.

℠ *Chorus:*

God is___ great, but some - times life___ ain't good. And when I___ pray, it does-n't

al - ways turn out like___ I think___ it should,___ but I do it an - y - way.___

To Coda ⊕

sing,_____ I dream,_____ I love_____

an-y-way._____

HOME

Words and Music by
MICHAEL BUBLÉ, AMY FOSTER-GILLIES
and ALAN CHANG

Home - 6 - 1

Em7   D6   Cmaj9   D

I've___ had my run,___ and, ba-by, I'm done.___ I'm com-ing back

G   Bm/D D   G   Bm7   Em7   D6

home.___   Let me go home._____   It-'ll be al -

Freely

Cmaj9   D(4)   G

right,___ I'll be home to-night.___ I'm com-ing back___ home._____

JUST GOT STARTED LOVIN' YOU

Words and Music by
D. VINCENT WILLIAMS, JIM FEMINO
and JAMES OTTO

Verses 1 & 2:

1. You don't have to go now, hon-ey, call 'em, tell 'em you won't be in to-day.___
2. What's the point in fight-in' what we're feel-in'? We both know we'll nev-er win.___

Ba - by, there ain't noth-in' at the of - fice so im-por-tant it can't
Ain't this what we're miss-in'? Let's just stop all this re-sist-in' and give

Repeat ad lib. and fade

LOST IN THIS MOMENT

Words and Music by
JOHN RICH, RODNEY CLAWSON
and KEITH ANDERSON

1. I see your ma-ma and the can-dles and the tears and ro - ses.

I see your dad-dy walk his daugh-ter down the aisle.

And my knees start to trem-ble as I tell the preach-er, "Don't she look beau-ti-ful

Lost in This Moment - 5 - 1

Verses 2 & 3:

2. All the won-der-ful___ words   in my head I've been___ think-ing,___
3. *See additional lyrics*

you know, I wan-na say them all   just   right.___

I lift your veil, and an-gels___ start   sing-ing.___   Such a heav - en - ly___

22

Verse 3:
I smell the jasmine floating in the air like a love song,
Watch my words draw sweet tears from your eyes.
Bow our heads while the preacher talks to Jesus,
Please bless this brand-new life, yeah.
(To Chorus:)

Gtr. tuned down 1/2 step:
⑥ = E♭ ③ = G♭
⑤ = A♭ ② = B♭
④ = D♭ ① = E♭

LAST NAME

Words and Music by
CARRIE UNDERWOOD, HILLARY LINDSEY
and LUKE LAIRD

Moderately slow country rock ♩ = 80

Verses 1 & 2:

1. Last night, I got served a lit-tle bit too much of that poi-son, ba-by.
2. We left the club right a-round three o'-clock in the morn-ing. His

Last night, I did things I'm not proud of, and I got a lit-tle cra-zy.
Pin - to sit-tin' there in the park-ing_____ lot, well, it should-'ve been a warn-ing.

...end solo)

Verse 3:

3. To-day, I woke up think-in' 'bout El-vis, some-where in Ve-gas. I'm not sure

how I got here or how this ring on my left hand just ap-peared___ out of

no-where. I got-ta go. I take the chips and the Pin - to and hit the road.__ They say what

LOVE DON'T LIVE HERE

Words and Music by
DAVID WESLEY HAYWOOD,
CHARLES KELLEY and HILLARY SCOTT

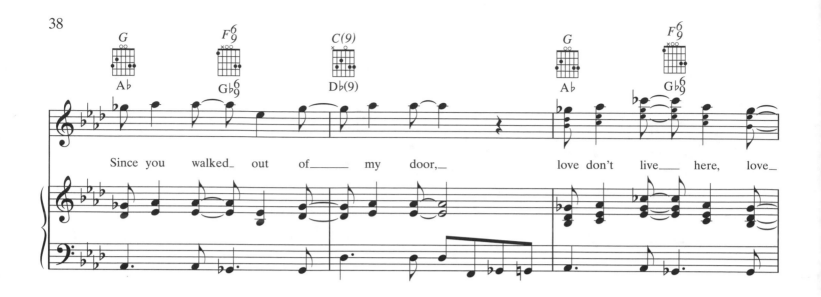

Since you walked_ out of _____ my door,_ love don't live_ here, love_

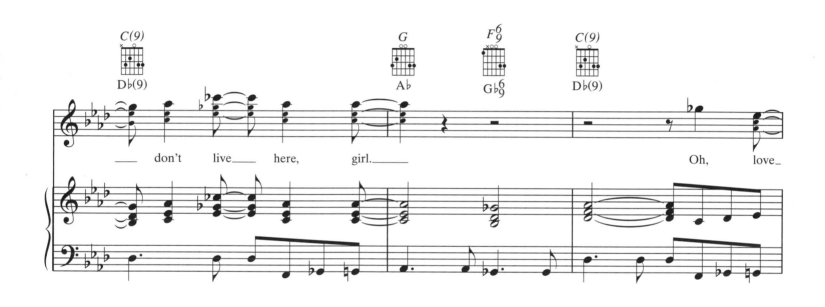

_____ don't live_____ here, girl._____ Oh, love_

_____ don't live_____ here an - y - more._____

STRONGER WOMAN

Words and Music by
MARV GREEN and
JEWEL KILCHER

Stronger Woman - 5 - 1

Verse 2:
The light bulbs buzz, I get up,
Head to my drawer.
Wish there was more I could say,
Another fairy tale fades to grey.
I've lived on hope, like a child,
Walking that mile, faking that smile,
All the while, wishing my heart had wings.
Well, from now on, I'm gonna be
The kind of woman I'd want my daughter to be.
(To Chorus:)

MARGARITAVILLE

Words and Music by
JIMMY BUFFETT

Moderately ♩ = 120

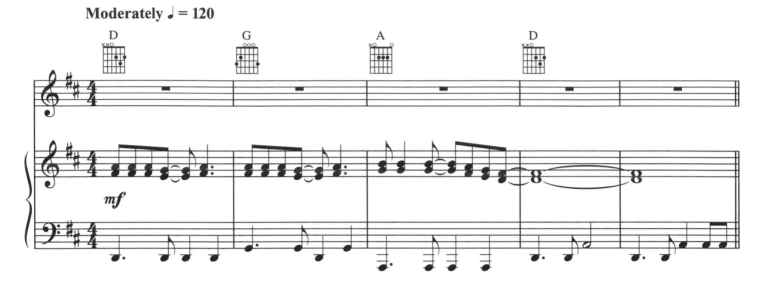

Verse:

1. Nib - blin' on sponge - cake, watch - in' the sun___
2. Don't know the rea - son I stayed here all sea -
3. I blew out my flip - flop, stepped on a pop -

___ bake; all of those tour - ists cov - ered with oil.___
son with noth - ing to show___ but this brand - new tat - too.___
top; cut my heel,___ had to cruise on back home.___

Margaritaville - 4 - 1

Chorus:

Wast-in' a-way a-gain in Mar-ga-ri-ta-ville,

SO SMALL

Words and Music by
CARRIE UNDERWOOD, HILLARY LINDSEY
and LUKE LAIRD

So Small - 8 - 1

THAT SONG IN MY HEAD

Words and Music by
WENDELL MOBLEY, JIM COLLINS
and TONI MARTIN

That Song in My Head - 5 - 1

C/E F G Am
Start-ed sling-in' that air___ gui - tar,___ man, you sure can___ play.______ And I've
C C/E F G G/B C
had___ that song___ in my head all___ day.______ I don't know_ who sings_
Chorus:
F G C
___ it. I keep search - in' the ra - di - o.______ I just wan - na hear_
f
F G Am G
___ it so I can watch that vid - e - o______ I got___ in my

Verse 3:
I said, "How 'bout an autograph for ya, your biggest fan?"
You wrote your name and your number in the palm of my hand.
My heart and that big bass speaker were thumpin' away.
And I've had that song in my head all day.
(To Chorus:)